Keto Chaffle Diet

Try Out 50 Keto Chaffle Recipes, Boost
Your Metabolism And Lose Weight

Table of Contents

INTRODUCTION

With a growing concern for healthy eating across the Globe, there are plenty of advanced and fancy diets available in the market. People approach nutritionists to learn about the various diet plans and their benefits and side effects. The main priority of these diets is weight loss and many nutritionists have started working on making new meal plans and guiding people about how these diets can be effective. They seem to be managing it very well.

The ketogenic diet generally referred to as the keto diet, is one of those diets that has earned a lot of praise from people around the globe, especially from those who have lost weight through it.

This diet plan, endorsed by celebrities, and supported by nutritionists, has been successful in gaining mass acceptance.

This book was written especially for those interested to explore and take advantage of this easy and interesting method of dieting. This book constitutes up to 50 delicious recipes so that you don't find your diet boring while upholding the rules of healthy eating. Who says diet is bland and boring? Keep reading and you'll be amazed!

WHAT IS THE KETO CHAFFLE DIET?

Those who are unfamiliar with this term, the ketogenic chaffle diet consists of increasing healthy fat consumption (avocado, olive oil, nuts, etc.) and reducing carbohydrate consumption (root vegetables, squash, rice, bread, pasta, etc.). The liver then produces ketone bodies; this phenomenon is called ketosis.

For those who need to ponder how much weight is lost through this. One reason for that is ketosis. When the body is in ketosis, it uses its fat to provide the body with energy for metabolic processes because the body is deprived of the carbohydrates that are an instant energy source.

You won't feel hungry between meals by taking fat and avoiding carbohydrates.

With an already-increasing number of people opting for the ketogenic chaffle diet, the nutritionists appear to be more interested in discovering different approaches to adding carbohydrates to the meal plan while also taking care of ketosis. Fortunately, keto bloggers are constantly thinking about innovative ways of appreciating relatively common foods, even while remaining within the best possible carb and sugar consumption plan.

Keto plans for protein bars, fat bombs, bagels, wraps, treats, and even sweets, similar to pumpkin or walnut pie, are all available on the internet.

This is the best part that you can even modify your diet. We strongly accept that you can never have an excessive number of keto makeovers of your favorite convenience foods, so the web has now honored us with a keto waffle formula.

The question is what is chaffle? It is a waffle made with cheddar and eggs that lets keto calorie counters sink to a warm, delicious early lunch waffle. A commendable model from Karly Campbell, a blogger over at That Low Carb Life, has introduced an innovative recipe of making a chaffle by using one big size egg and 1/2 a cup of finely chopped mozzarella cheese. Utilizing a small waffle maker, this formula yields precisely two chaffles.

Keeping in mind the basic rule of the keto diet, the waffle's base is cheddar — not a grain — and that is what makes it keto-accommodating. There is room for innovation. To make the base of the chaffle you should use those food items which can provide a strong base and make a perfect shape of the waffle, mozzarella or cheddar is perfect stuff. You can also add almond flour to the surface, which makes the waffle more "bready" and eliminates the eggy taste.

You can bring new ideas for seasonings and toppings of the chaffle. For example toss on some avocado, put an egg on it, transform two chaffles into a burger bun! Enjoy your meal while staying in a keto diet.

You must be thinking about why it is called a chaffle. The main ingredient in making a chaffle is cheese. So it is called as Chaffle and not waffle. This book is for all the waffle lovers who are opting for a keto diet because now they don't need to compromise on their waffle cravings. You can say that chaffles are cheese waffles. This sounds interesting!

The Chaffles are free of flour while the main ingredient used to make waffles is flour. Eggs and cheese are primary ingredients in making chaffles. You can call it a low-carb waffle heck. Those people who have been following this diet are drooling over this recipe. You can easily fix your waffle by choosing the keto chaffle diet.

This is a modified version of waffle but the best part is you can enjoy your diet without thinking about the carbs because it is a low-carb recipe. You can try so many combinations while dressing up the chaffles keeping the keto diet in mind. Thus those who crave some waffles and are on a diet can enjoy their modified waffles easily.

WHO SHOULD TAKE A KETO CHAFFLE DIET?

Following is a brief discussion of the effectiveness of the ketogenic chaffle diet in different diseases:

Effectiveness Against Epilepsy

The role of the ketogenic chaffle diet in epilepsy management is well proven. About half of the prescribed children have reduced the frequency of their seizures, up to 50%. Additionally, the ketogenic chaffle diet is followed by an improvement in behavior, attention, memory, and academic progress, these results may be associated with a decrease in antiepileptic drugs. The keto chaffle diet is less opted by the adult epileptic patients.

The recent synopsis of 17 small studies (conducted on 3 to 87 patients) confirms that it reduces seizures in responder patients (by at least 50 percent) and implies that it helps to improve mood and quality of life.

Effectiveness For Weight Loss

The ketogenic chaffle diet helps in weight loss as long as you control energy intake. The synopsis of 13 studies, gathering just over 1400 patients, concludes that the ketogenic chaffle diet is better than a classic weight loss diet in which lipids only provide 30 percent of calories: after 1 year of monitoring, the weight loss achieved was nearly 1 kilogram higher.

A similar study was published in 2016 which suggested that people on a ketogenic chaffle diet lost 12.5 kg and 11.6 cm in the waist after 2 years of follow-up, while people on a classic diet lost only 4 kilos and 4.1 cm in the waist.

As with all weight-loss diets, the question arises of maintaining the weight after following the diet for the short or long-term. In a study of 377 obese people followed for 1 year, the ketogenic chaffle diet helped lose an average of 12 kilos in the first 12 weeks, then the weight was maintained during the following 40 weeks.

Due to limited research done on the association between keto chaffle diet and weight management, the researchers are unable to affirm whether the ketogenic chaffle diet allows excess pounds to be definitively eliminated. Moreover, data on their safety are lacking beyond 1 year.

The ketogenic chaffle diet helps control appetite and promote the burning of fat reserves, as per recent studies, but should be used for short periods (for example, for 20 days), alternating with a calorie-deficit diet form to allow healthy weight loss. They also highlight the importance of weight gain prevention and reintroduction of carbohydrates only gradually after a ketogenic chaffle diet.

Type-2 Diabetes

Researchers are debating the role of the ketogenic chaffle diet in managing Type 2 diabetes. This type of diabetes is associated with insulin resistance, the efficiency of the insulin produced by the pancreas is reduced and consequently, a level of blood sugar that remains too high, especially in the hours after meals. In most cases, insulin resistance is due to extra fat located in the abdomen.

The treatment involves weight loss for most people with type 2 diabetes which reduces insulin resistance and thus improves blood sugar control.

For a short period, the keto chaffle diet can be really helpful and it can be a good strategy for those individuals whose main goal is to lose weight as it provides few carbohydrates (less than 50 g per day), it does not risk 'increasing blood sugar levels despite insulin resistance." A study was carried out in Spain on a group of 90 overweight types 2 diabetics, men and women between the ages of 30 and 65, which compared the two groups. one group was on a low-calorie classic diet while the other was put on to a keto chaffle diet. The group on a ketogenic chaffle diet lost an average of nearly 15 kilos after 4 months, compared to the group on a classic diet that lost only a few kilos.

In the ketogenic group, glycated hemoglobin (HbA1c), which tells about the blood glucose levels during the 3 months preceding the assay, further decreased from 6.9% to 6%.

The diets low in carbohydrates (but not necessarily as low in carbohydrates as the ketogenic chaffle diet) are the most efficient in blood sugar regulation of type 2 diabetics, as per some researchers, who have gathered existing studies.

However, the official recommendations of learned societies are not heading in that direction.

The American Diabetes Association recommends maintaining at least 150 g of carbohydrates per day, while the Francophone Diabetes Society recommends consuming 45 to 55 percent of calories of carbohydrates. A review of studies on the subject conducted by a group of American researchers in 2018 confirms that low-carbohydrate diets ensure full blood sugar control, but that high-carbohydrate and low-fat diets, on the other hand, are more effective in reducing cardiovascular risk factors (diabetes is a major risk factor in the development of the cardiovascular diseases).

The role of the keto chaffle diet in the management of type 2 diabetes is still not clear.

It is advised not to opt for a keto chaffle diet if you are suffering from ane metabolic disorder or if your organs do not function properly.

Parkinson's Disease

In the management of Parkinson's disease, the role of the keto chaffle diet has been studied. The rodents were subjected to this diet and the study suggested that it prevents the degeneration of neurons producing dopamine. Dopamine is a chemical whose deficiency leads to Parkinson's disease.

A small group of patients conducted few studies in humans, and the results were found to be encouraging.

The ketogenic chaffle diet is found to be effective in improving access to vocabulary and memory, as well as non-motor symptoms such as depression, fatigue, daytime sleepiness, and urinary problems.

The researchers have gathered all the results of the recent studies done. these studies also include patients suffering from Alzheimer's disease.

Their report supported the beneficial role of the keto chaffle diet in the prevention of neurological disease.

 but more research is required to support this report. The researchers also pointed out the fact that the patients who were involved were generally old and it is advised to opt for keto chaffle diet with great care and knowledge.

Like other diets the keto chaffle diet has also some benefits and side effects like suppression of appetite because of which people eat less. the old people should be aware of all the risk factors as the metabolism is different in old people.

Cancers

The role of the keto chaffle diet has also been studied in the management of cancer.

Those diseases that are usually accompanied by insulin resistance, which impedes the body's proper use of carbohydrates, and thus promotes weight loss and weakening.

The role of keto chaffle diet in the management of cancer is explained in a way that as the cancer cells require a huge amount of carbohydrates for their growth since the keto chaffle diet is based on low-carbs it will not provide sufficient carbohydrates to the tumor cells and it will promote their apoptosis (cell death). More research is required to support this reason.

Researchers from the National Food Cancer Research Network (NACRe) carried out a study in 2017 studying the relationship between restrictive diets or fasting and management of cancer. The study suggested that the ketogenic chaffle diet was found to be effective in the reduction of growth of the tumor in the majority of laboratory studies in mice.

They concluded that: "the available data is insufficient and do not provide any evidence of the ketogenic chaffle diet's interest in preventing human cancers."

In 2018 other researchers also gathered different studies testing the human ketogenic chaffle diet. Limited research is done and more research is required to determine the effect of the ketogenic chaffle diet on cancer prognosis, nutritional status, and patients ' health status more broadly.

FOLLOW A MODERATE KETOGENIC CHAFFLE DIET

Want to adopt a ketogenic chaffle diet, but that seems too hard for you? This diet is famous among celebrities. So follow the diet outline and prepare delicious meals and snacks that are rich in healthy fats. Fortunately, some variations of the keto chaffle diet, which are a little more versatile and mild, have been created. And your meal schedule can be adjusted accordingly.

Possible variations of the keto chaffle diet
Keep in mind that the keto chaffle diet puts the body in ketosis. In this metabolic state, as the principal source of fuel, you burn fat (rather than carbohydrates).

This supports weight loss and fat loss. Your body will get into ketosis with a modified diet and you can still lose weight and fat. A ketogenic chaffle diet is thus high in fat, mild in protein, and exceptionally low in carbohydrates. After a few days or weeks of such a diet, the body and brain become efficient in burning fat and ketones in place of carbohydrates.

The staple foods of a ketogenic chaffle diet include meat, fish, butter, eggs, cheese, heavy cream, oils, nuts, avocados, seeds, and low-carbon vegetables. Almost all sources of carbohydrates including wheat, rice, beans, potatoes, sweets, milk are removed from the diet.

In one study, people lost 2.2 times more weight on a ketogenic chaffle diet than those on a low-calorie, low-fat diet. The levels of triglyceride and HDL cholesterol also improved. Other studies show the ketogenic chaffle diet can help you lose weight and retain muscle mass. What are the diet variants?

The standard ketogenic chaffle diet
It contains 75% fat, 15-20% protein, and 5-10% carbohydrates. The meal plan is constructed with including fats like avocados, butter, ghee, oily fish and meats, olives, and extra virgin olive oil, in the standard ketogenic chaffle diet.

You need to get around 150 grams of fat per day to boost your slow metabolism so it's going to burn fat as fuel.

At the same time, you need to cut your carbohydrates to no more than 50, from around 300 grams a day.

You can only consume leafy vegetables, non-starchy vegetables, and low-carb fruits such as berries and melons. With-meal, you'll need to eat a reasonable amount of protein, about 90 grams a day, or 30 grams.

The targeted ketogenic chaffle diet
Targeted diet is famous among athletes and active individuals living a keto lifestyle but having more carbohydrates. It contains 65% to 70% fat, 20% protein and 10 % to 15% carbohydrates.

Individuals can consume 20 to 30 grams of extra carbohydrates before and after the workouts.

This helps in weight loss and better recovery. The best options are fruits, dairy, cereal or fruit-based foods, or sports nutrition products. The carbohydrates are not stored as body fat since extra carbohydrates are burned quickly.

The cyclical ketogenic chaffle diet
This diet consists of 75% fat, 15-20% protein, 5-10% carbohydrates during ketogenic days and 25% fat, 25% protein, and 50% carbohydrates throughout rest days. This diet has some peculiar characteristics. This type of diet comprises 5 days of traditional ketogenic chaffle diet and 2 days per week without a ketogenic diet. During their day of rest, some people choose a few events: holidays, birthdays, and special occasions.

This type of diet is a way of getting into and out of ketosis while enjoying a balanced diet in the days of rest. For best results, eat healthy, high-carb foods during rest days. Select fruits, starchy vegetables, dairy products, and whole grains (instead of adding sugars or highly processed foods).

Keto-protein diet
You'll need to make up your meal plan with 60-65 percent fat, 30 percent protein, and 5-10 percent carbohydrates in this diet.

Many people find it easier to adopt this adapted keto chaffle diet because it helps you to consume more protein and less fat than the regular keto chaffle diet. This plan includes eating 120 grams of protein a day.

Proteins and fats can be adjusted with 113 grams of meat, fish, or poultry, and around 130 grams of fat per day. Carbohydrates are always limited to less than 10% of the calories per day.

The method, however, does not lead to ketosis. Proteins can also be converted to glucose in this diet, just as carbohydrates do. The great news is that a high protein ketogenic diet usually often contributes to weight loss.

The question that which is the best diet to lose weight or maintain a healthy weight is still unanswered. Consult your nutritionist at all times, before choosing which one is right for you.

DOES THE KETOGENIC CHAFFLE DIET ALLOW YOU TO LOSE WEIGHT?

As described by Professor Cynober, this sort of extreme diet helps you lose weight. In one month the person will lose a few the issue with such strict diets is a rebound effect. People also tend to gain more weight than they had previously lost. The common" yo-yo "effect is seen in all diets. Dr. François Jornayvaz, head of the diabetology unit at the Geneva University Hospitals and author of many research publications on the ketogenic chaffle diet explained that studies conducted are suggestive of the fact that diets low in sugars allow a faster weight loss than diets low in fat. But in the long run, the weight curves match.

As per the doctor, this diet-where carbohydrates are virtually removed-must be differentiated from diets low in sugar. The doctor further explained that there are reasons to believe that moderately low-carbohydrate diets that do not exceed 1 gram of sugar per day may be beneficial, especially for patients with diabetes. But it is important to make sure that the right form of fat is consumed. Vegetable fat is preferred over the animal fat. Otherwise, there is a risk that fatty liver and hypercholesterolemia can develop, with long-term harmful effects. Although the role of keto chaffle diet in weight loss and management of diseases like cancer, diabetes, Alzheimer's, and Parkinson's is positive. It must be recalled that its efficacy has only been clinically proven in epilepsy.

Are there any side effects?

According to Professor Luc Cynober switching from a conventional diet to a ketogenic chaffle diet in the short term can lead to nausea, constipation, fatigue, headaches, cramps, and bad breathing. These are all the mainly dehydration related inconveniences. The body is compelled to use its glucose reserves while following this diet. However, glucose is stored in the muscle with water. Hence, its use leads to the elimination of water, which contributes to weight loss but also dehydration.

This diet limits the intake of fruits and vegetables and this can also lead to deficiencies. "Vitamin, mineral, and fiber deficiencies may be present," says Professor Cynober.

Therefore you need to take advice from a dietitian or a nutritionist before embarking on such a type of diet. The effects, in the long run, are poorly understood. The significant proportion of the experimental work that has been done so far has concentrated on a small number of participants and/or does not include a comparative control group. Dr. Jornayvaz explained that they have the best evidence from children with epilepsy. They show that the risk of developing kidney stones, osteoporosis, and a growth disorder eventually exists. To become a healthy individual it is required to consume a balanced diet. Consuming fats in large quantities and removing carbohydrates completely from the body is not recommended.

The National Food Safety Agency (ANSES) recalled in a report on weight loss diets released in 2010 that "the search for weight loss without formal medical guidance involves risks, especially when practices are used and unbalanced and poorly diversified food is consumed. They further added that nothing can replace a balanced, diversified diet from a health perspective, ensuring that the daily intake of energy does not exceed the needs.

BOOST YOUR METABOLISM NATURALLY WITH THE KETO DIET

The body has three types of food fuels: carbohydrates, fats, and proteins to function. The liver starts to produce ketone bodies from dietary fat or body fat stores when carbohydrates are in very short supply-as is the case with the ketogenic chaffle diet-as well.

It's said that when the body is in "ketosis": it turns into a "burn" fat machine. Therefore ketones become the primary source of energy for most of our cells. This change occurs between two and four days on average after the plan is adopted.

Lipids produce 35-40% of calories in a healthy balanced diet, carbohydrates 40-55%, and proteins 10-20%. Consequently, the ketogenic chaffle diet implies a change in eating habits. It also needs to be followed very rigorously (providing very few carbohydrates) to produce ketone bodies and thus be efficient.

The presence of ketones in the body is routinely tested by urinalysis when treated for epilepsy. The ketogenic chaffle diet causes profound changes in the body:

The ketone bodies on expiration give a different breath and these include acetone, acetoacetate, and beta-hydroxybutyrate and are not produced in the context of a traditional food supplying carbohydrates (in the form of bread, starchy foods, fruits, etc.).

However, ketone bodies, especially beta-hydroxybutyrate, appear to have a protective effect on neurons, especially by exercising antioxidant activity. They also have an anti-convulsant function, which may clarify their involvement in reducing epileptic seizures. Laboratory experiments also indicate that they prevent degeneration of the nerve cells that contain dopamine, which seeks the attention of researchers working on Parkinson's disease (a neurological disorder caused by dopamine deficiency). Ketones also exert an appetite suppressant effect that contributes to the ketogenic chaffle diet's weight loss effect.

This diet decreases insulin production. This hormone, the production of which is triggered by the rise in glycemia (level of blood sugar), is used to regulate blood sugar levels but also to store carbohydrates and lipids and to avoid the use of fat reserves as a fuel. The ketogenic diet of the chaffle, which provides carbohydrates in small quantities, is followed by a low insulin level which allows the mobilization and burning of fat reserves.

This is the reason why the role of this diet in the management of weight is appreciated. Indeed, some researchers have attributed the global "obesity epidemic" to excessive consumption of ultra-processed industrial foods with a high glycemic index:

Whose carbohydrates are quickly digested and excessively increase blood sugar levels, and consequently insulin. Also in the management of type 2 diabetes, the most common form of diabetes accompanied by insulin resistance, the ketogenic chaffle diet is being tested.

50 HEALTHY & LOW-CARB KETOGENIC RECIPES

BREAKFAST

1. Simple Chaffle

Prep time: 5 minutes | Cook time: 14 minutes | Serves: 2

Ingredients:

- ½ cup thinly sliced cheddar cheese
- 1 small egg, beaten

Instructions:

1. Preheat the waffle iron.
2. Open the iron and lay 1/8 of the cheddar cheese in the waffle, top with half of the egg, and then another 1/8 of the cheese.
3. Close and cook until crispy, 5 to 7 minutes.
4. Remove onto a plate and cool further.

5. Make a second chaffle with the remaining ingredients in the same manner. Enjoy your meal!

Nutrition Facts per Serving

- Calories 138
- Fats 7.19g
- Carbs 7.65g
- Net Carbs 7.65g
- Protein 10.68g

2. Zucchini-Parsley Chaffles

Prep time: 10-min | Cook time: 28 minutes |

Serves: 4

Ingredients:

- 2 small zucchinis (grated), 1 large egg (beaten)
- ½ cup finely grated mozzarella cheese
- 2 tbsp finely grated Parmesan cheese
- 1/8 tsp dried basil
- 1/8-tsp freshly ground black pepper

Instructions:

1. Preheat the waffle iron.
2. Using a medium bowl, mix all the ingredients.
3. Open the iron, pour in a quarter cup of the mixture, close the iron, and cook for 6 to 7 minutes or until crispy.

4. Remove the chaffle, plate, and set aside.

5. Make the three more chaffles in the same manner, using the remaining ingredients. Allow cooling and serve after.

Nutrition Facts per Serving

- Calories 58
- Fats 4.06g
- Carbs 1.36g
- Net Carbs 1.16g
- Protein 4g

3. Creamy Rich Chaffles

Prep time: 5 minutes | Cook time: 28

minutes | Serves: 4

Ingredients:

- 1 egg, beaten
- ½ cup shredded mozzarella cheese 2 tbsp almond flour
- 1 tbsp cream cheese, softened
- ¾ tsp baking powder
- 3 tbsp water

Instructions:

1. Preheat the waffle iron.
2. Take a medium bowl, mix all the ingredients.
3. Open the iron, pour in a quarter cup of the mixture, close the iron, and cook for 6 to 7 minutes or until crispy.
4. Remove the chaffle, plate, and set aside.

5. Make three more chaffles, in the same manner, using the remaining ingredients.
6. Allow cooling and serve after.

Nutrition Facts per Serving
- Calories 98
- Fats 4.54g
- Carbs 1.98g
- Net Carbs 1.38g
- Protein 12.38g

4. Light Parmesan Chaffles

Prep time: 10-min | Cook time: 28 minutes |

Serves: 4

Ingredients:

- 1 egg, beaten
- ½ tsp ground flaxseed
- ¼ tsp baking powder
- 1/3 cup finely grated cheddar cheese
- ¼ cup finely grated Parmesan cheese

Instructions:

1. Preheat the waffle iron.
2. By using a medium bowl, mix all the ingredients except the Parmesan cheese.
3. Open the iron and sprinkle a little of the Parmesan cheese in the bottom. Pour on ¼ cup of the mixed ingredients and top with a little more of the Parmesan cheese.

4. Close the iron and cook until crispy, 6 to 7 minutes.

5. Remove the chaffle onto a plate and set aside.

6. Make three more chaffles using the remaining ingredients in the same manner. Allow cooling and serve after.

Nutrition Facts per Serving

- Calories 119
- Fats 5.62g
- Carbs 7.36g
- Net Carbs 7.26g
- Protein 9.72g

5. Bacon Swiss Chaffles

Prep time: 5 minutes | Cook time: 28 minutes | Serves: 4

Ingredients:

- 1 egg, beaten
- 1 tbsp finely chopped cooked bacon
- ½ cup finely grated Swiss cheese

Instructions:

1. Preheat the waffle iron.
2. By using a medium bowl, mix all the ingredients.
3. Open the iron, pour in a quarter of the mixture, cover, and cook until crispy, 6 to 7 minutes.
4. Remove the chaffle onto a plate.
5. Make three more chaffles using the remaining ingredients. Allow cooling and serve after.

Nutrition Facts per Serving

- Calories 82
- Fats 5.85g
- Carbs 2.1g
- Net Carbs 2.0g
- Protein 5.41g

6. Sandwich Bread Chaffles

Prep time: 10-min | Cook time: 28 minutes |

Serves: 4

Ingredients:

- 1 egg, beaten
- ½ cup finely grated Swiss cheese 4 tbsp mayonnaise
- 3 tbsp almond flour
- ¼ tsp baking powder 2 tsp water
- 2 tsp maple syrup

Instructions:

1. Preheat the waffle iron.
2. By using a medium bowl, mix all the ingredients until smooth batter forms.
3. Open the iron, pour in a quarter of the mixture, cover, and cook until crispy, 6 to 7 minutes.

4. Remove the chaffle onto a plate and set aside.
5. Make three more chaffles using the remaining ingredients.
6. Allow cooling and use for sandwiches.

Nutrition Facts per Serving

- Calories 85
- Fats 7.31g
- Carbs 0.96g
- Net Carbs 0.66g
- Protein 3.85g

7. Savory Broccoli Chaffles

Prep time: 10 minutes | Cook time: 28

minutes |Serves: 4

Ingredients:

- 1 cup riced broccoli
- ¼ tsp salt
- ¼ tsp freshly ground black pepper to taste
- ¼ tsp garlic powder
- ½ tsp Italian seasoning 1 egg, beaten
- ½ cup finely grated mozzarella cheese
- ½ cup finely grated Parmesan cheese

Instructions:

1. Preheat the waffle iron.
2. By using a medium bowl, mix all the ingredients except the Parmesan cheese.
3. Open the iron and sprinkle1/8 of the Parmesan cheese in the bottom.

4. Pour on ¼ cup of the mixed ingredients and top with 1/8 of the Parmesan cheese.
5. Close the iron and cook until crispy, 6 to 7 minutes.
6. Remove the chaffle onto a plate and set aside.
7. Make three more chaffles using the remaining ingredients in the same manner.
8. Allow cooling and serve after.

Nutrition Facts per Serving
- Calories 90
- Fats 3.79g
- Carbs 6.68g
- Net Carbs 5.88g
- Protein 7.63g

8. Apple Pie Chaffles

Prep time: 10-min | Cook time: 14 minutes |

Serves: 2

Ingredients:

- ½ cup finely grated mozzarella cheese 1 egg, beaten
- ¼ tsp apple pie spice
- 4 butter slices for serving

Instructions:

1. Preheat the waffle iron.
2. Open the iron, pour in half of the mozzarella cheese in the iron, top with half of the egg, and sprinkle with half of the apple pie spice.
3. Close the iron and cook until crispy, 6 to 7 minutes.
4. Remove the chaffle onto a plate and set aside.

5. Make the second chaffle with the remaining ingredients. Allow cooling and serve after.

Nutrition Facts per Serving

- Calories 146
- Fats 14.73g
- Carbs 0.9g
- Net Carbs 0.7g
- Protein 3.07g

9. Cinnamon-Mozzarella Chaffles

Prep time: 10-min | Cook time: 14 minutes | Serves: 2

Ingredients:

- egg, beaten
- ½ cup finely grated mozzarella cheese
- ½ tsp baking powder 1 tbsp vanilla extract

1 tbsp almond flour

- ½ tsp cinnamon powder

Instructions:

1. Preheat the waffle iron.
2. By using a medium bowl, mix all the ingredients until smooth batter forms.
3. Open the iron, pour in half of the mixture, cover, and cook until crispy, 6 to 7 minutes.
4. Remove the chaffle onto a plate and set aside.

5. Make the second chaffle with the remaining ingredients.

6. Allow cooling and enjoy.

Nutrition Facts per Serving

- Calories 56
- Fats 3.36g
- Carbs 1.85g
- Net Carbs 1.45g
- Protein 3.02g

10. Peanut Butter Chaffles

Prep time: 10-min | Cook time: 28 minutes |

Serves: 4

Ingredients:

- tbsp. sugar-free peanut butter powder 2 tbsp maple (sugar-free) syrup
- 1 egg, beaten
- ½ cup finely grated mozzarella cheese
- ¼ tsp baking powder
- ¼ tsp peanut butter extract
- tbsp softened cream cheese

Instructions:

1. Preheat the waffle iron.

2. By using a medium bowl, mix all the ingredients until smooth.

3. Open the iron and pour in a quarter of the mixture.

4. Close the iron and cook until crispy, 6 to 7 minutes.

6. Remove the chaffle onto a plate and set aside.

6. Make three more chaffles with the remaining batter.

7. Allow cooling and serve after.

Nutrition Facts per Serving

- Calories 102
- Fats 5.31g
- Carbs 10.41g
- Net Carbs 9.91g
- Protein 4.08g

11. BLT Chaffle Sandwiches

Prep time: 10-min | Cook time: 28 minutes |

Serves: 2

Ingredients:

- 1 egg, beaten
- ½ cup finely grated mozzarella cheese 2 scallions, finely chopped
- ½ tsp Italian seasoning 2 bacon slices, cooked 2 lettuce leaves
- tomato slices
- 1 tbsp mayonnaise

Instructions:

1. Preheat the waffle iron.

2. Meanwhile, in a medium bowl, mix the egg, mozzarella cheese, scallions, and Italian seasoning.

3. Open the iron, pour a quarter of the mixture into the iron, close and cook until crispy, 6 to 7 minutes.

4. Remove the chaffle onto a plate and set aside.

5. Make three more chaffles with the remaining batter.

6. To assemble the sandwich: on one chaffle, layer one bacon slice, one lettuce leaf, one tomato slice, and top with half of the mayonnaise. Cover with another chaffle.

7. Make a second sandwich in the same manner and enjoy it after.

Nutrition Facts per Serving
- Calories 114
- Fats 9.53g
- Carbs 2.17g
- Net Carbs 1.57g
- Protein 5.06g

12. Everything Bagel Chaffles

Prep time: 10-min | Cook time: 28 minutes | Serves: 4

Ingredients:

- 1 egg, beaten
- ½ cup finely grated Parmesan cheese 1 tsp Everything
- Bagel seasoning

Instructions:

1. Preheat the waffle iron.
2. By using a medium bowl, mix all the ingredients.
3. Open the iron, pour in a quarter of the mixture, close, and cook until crispy, 6 to 7 minutes.
4. Remove the chaffle onto a plate and set aside.
5. Make three more chaffles, allow cooling, and enjoy after.

Nutrition Facts per Serving

- Calories 53
- Fats 1.55g
- Carbs 4.08g
- Net Carbs 4.08g
- Protein 5.38g

13. Blueberry Shortcake Chaffles

Prep time: 10-min | Cook time: 14 minutes | Serves: 2

Ingredients:

- 1 egg, beaten
- 1 tbsp cream cheese, softened
- ¼ cup finely grated mozzarella cheese

1/4 tsp baking powder

- 4 fresh blueberries
- 1 tsp blueberry extract

Instructions:

1. Preheat the waffle iron.

2. By using a medium bowl mix all the ingredients.

3. Open the iron, pour in half of the batter, close, and cook until crispy, 6 to 7 minutes.

4. Remove the chaffle onto a plate and set aside.

5. Make the other chaffle with the remaining batter.

6. Allow cooling and enjoy after.

Nutrition Facts per Serving

- Calories 46
- Fats 3.21g
- Carbs 1.16g
- Net Carbs 1.14g
- Protein 2.45g

14.   Raspberry-Pecan Chaffles

*Prep time: 10-min | Cook time: 14 minutes
| Serves: 2*

Ingredients:

- 1 egg, beaten
- ½ cup finely grated mozzarella cheese 1 tbsp cream cheese, softened
- tbsp sugar-free maple syrup
- ¼ tsp raspberry extract
- ¼ tsp vanilla extract
- tbsp sugar-free caramel sauce for topping 3 tbsp chopped pecans for topping

Instructions:

1. Preheat the waffle iron.
2. By using a medium bowl mix all the ingredients.
3. Open the iron, pour in half of the batter,

close, and cook until crispy, 6 to 7
minutes.

4. Remove the chaffle onto a plate and set
aside.

5. Make another chaffle with the
remaining batter.

6. To serve: drizzle the caramel sauce on
the chaffles and top with the pecans.

Nutrition Facts per Serving

- Calories 186
- Fats 16.3g
- Carbs 3.53g
- Net Carbs 2.23g
- Protein 7.43g

15. Pumpkin Spice Chaffles

Prep time: 10-min | Cook time: 14 minutes | Serves: 2

Ingredients:

- 1 egg, beaten
- ½ tsp pumpkin pie spice
- ½ cup finely grated mozzarella cheese

1 tbsp sugar-free pumpkin puree

Instructions:

1. Preheat the waffle iron.

2. By using a medium bowl mix all the ingredients.

3. Open the iron, pour in half of the batter, close, and cook until crispy, 6 to 7 minutes.

4. Remove the chaffle onto a plate and set aside.

5. Make another chaffle with the remaining batter.

6. Allow cooling and serve afterward.

Nutrition Facts per Serving

- Calories 90
- Fats 6.46g
- Carbs 1.98g
- Net Carbs 1.58g
- Protein 5.94g

16. Breakfast Spinach Ricotta Chaffles

Prep time: 10-min | Cook time: 28 minutes | Serves: 4

Ingredients:

● 4 oz frozen spinach, thawed, squeezed dry 1 cup ricotta cheese

● 2 eggs, beaten

● ½ tsp garlic powder

● ¼ cup finely grated Pecorino Romano cheese

● ½ cup finely grated mozzarella cheese

● Salt and freshly ground black pepper to taste

Instructions:

1. Preheat the waffle iron.
2. By using a medium bowl, mix all the ingredients.

3. Open the iron, lightly grease with cooking spray, and spoon in a quarter of the mixture.

4. Close the iron and cook until brown and crispy, 7 minutes.

5. Remove the chaffle onto a plate and set aside.

6. Make three more chaffles with the remaining mixture.

7. Allow cooling and serve afterward.

Nutrition Facts per Serving

- Calories 188
- Fats 13.15g
- Carbs 5.06g
- Net Carbs 4.06g
- Protein 12.79g

Prep time: 15-min | Cook time: 28 minutes | Serves: 4

Ingredients:

For the chaffles:

● 1 cup finely grated cheddar cheese 2 eggs, beaten

For the egg stuffing:

● 1 tbsp olive oil 4 large eggs, small green bell pepper, deseeded and chopped

● 1 small red bell pepper, deseeded and chopped Salt and freshly ground black pepper to taste tbsp grated Parmesan cheese

Instructions:

For the chaffles:

1. Preheat the waffle iron.

2. In a medium bowl, mix the cheddar cheese and egg.

3. Open the iron, pour in a quarter of the mixture, close, and cook until crispy, 6 to 7 minutes.

4. Plate and make three more chaffles using the remaining mixture.

 For the egg stuffing:

5. Meanwhile, heat the olive oil in a medium skillet over medium heat on a stovetop.

6. In a medium bowl, beat the eggs with the bell peppers, salt, black pepper, and Parmesan cheese.

7. Pour the mixture into the skillet and scramble until set to your likeness, 2 minutes.

8. Between two chaffles, spoon half of the scrambled eggs and repeat with the second set of chaffles.

9. Serve afterward.

Nutrition Facts per Serving:

- Calories 387
- Fats 22.52g
- Carbs 18.12g
- Net Carbs 17.52g
- Protein 27.76g

LUNCH

18. Simple Keto Chaffle Recipe

Prep time: 15-min | Cook time: 28 minutes |
Serves: 4

Ingredients:

- Shredded Cheese – you can use your preferred variety
- An Egg
- Pinch of Salt
- As usual, feel free to add in spices like Italian seasoning, garlic powder, curry powder, or smoked paprika.

Directions:

1. Preheat your mini waffle maker.
2. In a bowl, whisk your egg then add a pinch of salt and 1/2 cup of cheese.

3. Once your mini waffle maker is heated, pour 1/2 of the batter on the waffle maker.*

4. Allow the chaffle to cook for 2-3 minutes.

5. Cook the other half of the batter to make your second chaffle.

6. Set your chaffle on a wire rack for 2-3 minutes to allow it to firm up.

7. *Optional

8. You could sprinkle some cheese directly on the waffle maker, pour on the batter, then add a little more cheese on top. This creates a very crispy chaffle.

9. You could also add 2tbsp of almond flour to the batter if you want a more dense chaffle.

19. 2-Ingredient Chaffle

Prep time: 10-min | Cook time: 1 minute |
Serves: 4

Ingredients:

- Eggs
- 1 cup shredded cheese

Instructions:

1. In a small bowl, whisk together all ingredients. Pour the ingredients into a preheated waffle griddle.

2. Allow the waffle to cook for 45 seconds to one minute before closing the waffle maker. This will help prevent spillage.

3. Cook for about seven minutes or until golden brown.

20. Easy Recipe

Prep time: 10-min | Cook time: 25 minutes |
Serves: 4

Ingredients:

- 1 egg
- 1/2 cup shredded cheddar cheese

Instructions:

1. Start by heating up your waffle maker (or simply plugging it in).
2. Greasing your waffle maker is completely optional, I have found that it's not necessary.
3. In a small bowl crack one egg.
4. Then add in 1/2 cup shredded cheese.
5. Whisk the egg and cheese mixture until well combined.

6. Sprinkle a little cheese on the waffle maker before adding the mixture to the waffle maker and then also after adding the mixture.

7. Pour 1/2 the mixture into the Dash waffle maker OR all the mixture into a standard size waffle maker.

8. Cook for 3-4 minute until set and crispy. Let cool for a few minutes before enjoying.

21. Pumpkin Chaffle

Prep time: 10-min | Cook time: 28 minutes |
Serves: 4

Ingredients:

- 1/2 cup shredded mozzarella cheese 1
large egg
- tbsp pumpkin puree 1/2 tsp pumpkin spice
1/2 tsp cinnamon
- pinch stevia extract powder

Instructions:

1. Preheat your waffle maker.
2. In a bowl combine the pumpkin spice, cinnamon, stevia, and cheese and whisk together.
3. Add the pumpkin puree and egg, continue whisking until you have a well combined batter.

4. Pour half of the batter in the waffle maker and cook until done. (Cooking time depends on waffle maker.)
5. Let cool for 3 minutes before serving.

22. Cinnamon Apple Chaffle

Prep time: 15-min | Cook time: 18 minutes |

Serves: 4

Ingredients:

Vanilla Bean Sauce:

- ½ teaspoon monk fruit sweetener
- ½ teaspoon vanilla extract 1 egg yolk
- cup whipping cream
- tablespoon ghee or butter
- ounces cream cheese softened Vanilla bean whole

Chaffle:

- tablespoon coconut flour 1 teaspoon baking powder 2 teaspoons cinnamon
- ½ teaspoon monk fruit sweetener 3 large eggs
- ¼ cup granny smith apple skinned + diced (or 1 tablespoon natural erythritol apple flavoring)

- ¾ cup mozzarella cheese shredded
- ¼ cup mild cheddar cheese shredded

Instructions:

Vanilla Bean Sauce:

1. In a medium saucepan, add heavy whipping cream, ghee, and vanilla bean

2. Heat over medium high heat until just starting to boil, then add sweetener and lower heat and simmer for 10 minutes. Remove vanilla bean and scrape remaining vanilla seeds into whipping cream, then discard bean. Remove from heat and add in egg yolk while whisking vigorously. Stir in cream cheese until melted.

3. Put vanilla sauce in heat safe container and place in the fridge to cool. Apple Chaffle:

4. Preheat waffle maker and spray generously with low carb non-stick spray. In a large mixing bowl, add egg and beat until frothy.

5. Add vanilla and cheese and beat until well combined.

6. In a small mixing bowl, whisk together flour, baking powder, sweetener, and cinnamon.

7. Add dry ingredients to egg mixture and mix until just combined. Gently fold in diced apples.

8. Spray waffle maker with cooking spray.

9. Pour batter into waffle maker on medium, high heat and cook until starting to brown on the outside – about 4 minutes.

10. Cool "chaffle" slightly, then top with vanilla sauce.

Prep time: 10-min | Cook time: 28 minutes |
Serves: 4

Ingredients:

● canned organic mushroom, 5 tablespoons cheddar cheese

● ounces cream cheese softened 1 egg

Instructions:

1. Heat up waffle maker.

2. In a medium size bowl add the chicken, buffalo sauce, cheddar cheese, softened cream cheese, and egg.

3. Mix together until the mixture is well combined.

4. Spray your waffle maker with your favorite nonstick cooking spray. Sprinkle a little cheese on the bottom of the waffle maker.

5. Add the mixture to your waffle maker.
6. Then sprinkle a little cheese on the top of the mixture.
7. Cook for 3-5 minutes until chaffle is fully cooked and crispy

24. Keto Chocolate Chaffle Recipe

Prep time: 14-min | Cook time: 25 minutes |
Serves: 4

Ingredients:

- 1 tablespoon heavy whipping cream
- ½ teaspoon coconut flour
- ¼ teaspoon baking powder 1 large egg
- tablespoon unsweetened cocoa powder

Pinch of stevia extract powder

Instructions:

1. Preheat your waffle maker.
2. In a bowl add the egg, cocoa powder, stevia, coconut flour, baking powder, heavy whipping cream whisk it together.
3. Pour the batter in the waffle maker and cook until ready
4. Let it cool off for about 3 minutes, it will get firmer.

25. Taco Chaffle

Prep time: 10-min | Cook time: 28 minutes |
Serves: 4

Ingredients:

- tablespoons coconut flour 1 teaspoon baking powder
- ½ teaspoon Himalayan pink salt 3 large eggs
- ½ cup mozzarella cheese shredded
- ½ cup sharp cheddar cheese shredded + ¼ cup for topping
- ½ pound ground beef
- 2 teaspoon chili powder 1 teaspoon cumin
- 1 teaspoon paprika
- 1 teaspoon garlic powder
- ¼ cup sour cream
- 1 ripe avocado diced
- ½ cup tomato diced

- ½ cup romaine lettuce shredded

Instructions:

1. In a small mixing bowl, whisk together flour, baking powder, and salt. In a large mixing bowl, beat eggs until frothy.
2. Add cheese and beat until well combined and then add dry ingredients.
3. Preheat waffle maker to medium high heat and coat generously with low carb cooking spray.
4. Pour batter into waffle maker, close and cook for 4-5 minutes. Over medium high heat, brown ground beef.
5. Once beef is browned add ¼ cup of water and add seasonings.
6. Stir well and heat over low-medium for 7-9 minutes or until water is absorbed.

26. Simple Keto Chaffle

Prep time: 15-min | Cook time: 25 minutes |
Serves: 4

Ingredients:

- 1/2 C Shredded Cheddar Cheese 1 Egg
- Here's our simple recipe (makes 2):

Directions:

1. Sprinkle approx 1 Tablespoon Shredded Cheddar Cheese on your hot Chaffle maker. Mix 1 egg and 1/4 C Shredded Cheddar cheese. Pour half on top of the melted cheese

2. Sprinkle the remaining 1 Tablespoon Shredded Cheddar Cheese on top and cook your Chaffle until it stops steaming. Cook your second Chaffle using more cheese and the remaining egg mixture.

27. Jalapeno Popper Keto Chaffle

Prep time: 10-min | Cook time: 28 minutes |

Serves: 4

Ingredients:

- 1 tablespoon coconut flour, 1 teaspoon baking powder
- ¼ teaspoon Himalayan pink salt 4 slices bacon

large eggs

- 2-3 jalapeno peppers
- 8-ounces cream cheese
- cup sharp cheddar cheese, shredded

Instructions:

1. Wash, dry, & de-seed jalapeno peppers.
2. Dice one, slice the others.
3. In a pan on the stove, cook bacon until brown and crispy.
4. In a small mixing bowl, whisk together flour, baking powder, and salt. In a

mixing bowl, beat cream cheese until light and fluffy.

5. Preheat waffle maker and spray with low carb non-stick spray.

6. Take a mixing bowl, add egg and beat.

7. Add ½ cup cream cheese and the shredded cheese, then beat until well combined.

8. Add dry ingredients to egg mixture and beat until combined. Fold in diced jalapeno.

9. Pour batter into waffle maker on medium, high heat and cook until starting to brown on the outside – about 5 min.

10. Cool "chaffle" slightly, then top with the rest of the cream cheese, jalapeno slices, and crumbled bacon pieces. Serve and enjoy!

Prep time: 10-min | Cook time: 28 minutes |

Serves: 4

Ingredients:

- 1 Egg
- ⅓ C. Shredded cheddar cheese
- 1 ½ Tbsp. Heavy whipping cream 1 Tbsp. Almond flour
- Salt and pepper to taste Mini waffle iron

Instructions:

1. Heat up your mini waffle iron.
2. Mix the ingredients in a mixing bowl until well combined.
3. Place half of the batter mixture into the mini waffle maker, and cook for 3-5 minutes. Remove the first chaffle from the mini waffle iron, and place the other half of the batter in to cook.

29. Pumpkin Chaffles

Prep time: 12-min | Cook time: 25 minutes |

Serves: 4

Ingredients:

- 1/2 cup shredded mozzarella cheese 1

whole egg, beaten

- 1 1/2 tablespoons pumpkin purée
- 1/2 teaspoon Swerve confectioners
- 1/2 teaspoon vanilla extract
- 1/4 teaspoon Pumpkin Pie Spice
- 1/8 teaspoon pure maple extracts
- Optional: Roasted pecans, cinnamon,

whip cream and

- Sugar-Free Maple
- Syrup for topping

Instructions:

1. Turn on your Waffle Maker, and start preparing the batter.

2. Add in all the ingredients, except for the mozzarella cheese to a bowl and whisk. Add in the cheese and mix until well combined.

3. Spray your waffle plates with nonstick spray (I used coconut oil) and add in half the batter to the center. Close the lid and cook for 4-6 minutes, depending on how crispy you want your Chaffles.

4. Remove and cook the second Chaffle. Serve with all or any combination of toppings including butter, Sugar-Free Maple Syrup, roasted pecans, a dusting of ground cinnamon and a dollop of whip cream.

30. Jicama Hash Brown Chaffle Recipe

Prep time: 10-min | Cook time: 28 minutes |

Serves: 4

Ingredients:

- large jicama root
- 1/2 medium onion, minced f2 garlic

cloves, pressed

- 1f cup cheese of choice (I used Halloumi)
- eggs, whisked Salt and Pepper

Instructions:

1. Peel jicama
2. Shred in food processor
3. Place shredded jicama in a large colnder, sprinkle with 1-2 tsp of salt. Mix well and allow to drain.

4. Squeeze out as much li q uid as possible (very important step) Microwave for 5-8 minutes. Mix all ingredients.

5. Sprinkle a little cheese on waffle iron before adding 3 T of the mixture, sprinkle a little more cheese on top of the mixture

6. Cook for 5 minutes. Flip and cook 2 more. Top with a sunny side up egg! If you haven't experienced jicama in your dining repertoire, you have everything to gain — and if you're hoping to shed some extra pounds, this might be your new favorite.

31. Keto Chaffle Recipe

Prep time: 15-min | Cook time: 20 minutes |

Serves: 4

Ingredients:

- 1 large egg
- 1/2 c. shredded cheese Pinch of salt.

Seasoning to taste

Instructions:

1. Preheat the mini waffle maker. In a bowl- whisk the egg until beaten.

2. Shred the cheese. Add the cheese, salt and seasoning to the egg, then mix well. Scoop half of the mixture on the waffle maker spread evenly. Cook 3-4 minutes, until done to your liking (crispy). Pull it off and let it cool.

3. Add the rest of batter and cook the 2nd waffle. Enjoy!

32. Bacon- Jalapeño Chaffles

Prep time: 10-min | Cook time: 28 minutes |

Serves: 4

Ingredients:

- 1 egg, beaten
- ½ cup finely grated Gruyere cheese
- ¼ jalapeño pepper, deseeded and minced

2 tbsp finely chopped cooked bacon

Instructions:

1. Preheat the waffle iron.

2. By using a medium bowl mix all the ingredients.

3. Open the iron, pour in ¼ cup of the mixture, close the iron, and cook for 6 to 7 minutes or until crispy.

4. Remove the chaffle onto a plate and set aside.

5. Make three more chaffles using the remaining ingredients.

6. Allow cooling and serve after.

Nutrition Facts per Serving:

- Calories 83
- Fats 5.86g
- Carbs 2.37g
- Net Carbs 2.17g
- Protein 5.47g

33. Rich and Creamy Mini Chaffle

Prep time: 5minutes | Cooking time: 10 min

| Serve: 2

Ingredients:

- 2 eggs
- 1 cup mozzarella
- 2-tbsp Cream cheese
- 2-tbsp almond grinned
- ¾-tbsp baking powder
- 2-tbsp water

Direction:

1. Pre-heat a mini waffle iron
2. Then mix all the above-mentioned ingredients in a glass bowl
3. After that, grease your waffle iron
4. Cook in the mini waffle iron for at least 4 min
5. Serve warmly

34. Jalapeno Cheddar Chaffle

Preparation time: 10 min | cooking time:

4min | Serve: 2

Ingredients:

- 2 eggs
- ½- the cup of Cheddar cheese
- 16 slices Deli Jalapeno

Direction:

1. Heat a mini waffle maker
2. In a bowl, mix the eggs, cheddar cheese
3. Shred some of the cheddar cheese into the lower plate of the waffle maker
4. Then pour the mixture to the lower plate of the waffle maker
5. Sparkle the ground cheese again on the top with 4 slices of jalapeno and then close the lid
6. Cook for 4 min to get the crunch. Serve hot

DINNER

35. Chinese Chicken Chaffle

Prep Time:20-min | Total Time:30-min |

Serve: 2

Ingredients:

For the Chaffle:

- 2- Egg
- Mozzarella Cheese: 1- cup (shredded)
- Butter: 1- tbsp
- Almond flour: 2- tbsp
- Baking powder: ¼- tsp
- Salt: a- pinch

For the Chicken:

- Chicken pieces: -2-4
- Ginger powder: ½- tbsp
- Salt: ¼- tsp or as per your taste
- Black pepper: ¼- tsp or as per your taste

- Soy sauce: 1- tbsp
- Spring onion: 1- stalk

Instructions:

1. First boil the chicken in a saucepan, when done remove from water & pat dry shred the chicken into small pieces & add all the seasoning & spices. Then finely chop the spring onion & mix with the chicken & set aside Now preheat a mini waffle maker if needed & grease it

2. Then in a mixing bowl, add all the chaffle ingredients & mix well

3. Then pour a little amount of mixture to the lower plate of the waffle maker & spread it evenly to cover the plate properly

4. Now add the chicken mixture on top & again spread the thin layer of the mixture & close the lid

5. Now cook for at least 4 minutes to get the desired crunch then remove the chaffle from the heat

6. Finally, make as many chaffles as your mixture & waffle maker allow serve hot & enjoy.

Prep Time: 15-min | Total Time: 25-min |

Serve: 2

Ingredients:

- 2-Egg
- Cheddar cheese: 1½- cup
- Deli Jalapeno: 16- slices
- Boiled chicken: 1- cup (shredded)

Instructions:

1. First preheat a mini waffle maker if needed
2. Then in a mixing bowl, beat eggs & add chicken & half cheddar cheese to them
3. Now mix them all well
4. Then shred some of the remaining cheddar cheese to the lower plate of the waffle maker

5. Then pour the mixture to the shredded cheese

6. Now add the cheese again on the top with around 4 slices of jalapeno & close the lid

7. Then cook for at least 4 minutes to get the desired crunch Serve hot

8. Finally, make as many chaffles as your mixture allows

37. Chicken Stuffed Chaffles

Prep Time: 10-min | Total Time: 25-min |

Serve: 2

Ingredients:

For Chaffle:

- 2- Egg
- Mozzarella Cheese: ½- cup (shredded)
- Garlic powder: ¼- tsp
- Salt: ¼- tsp or as per your taste
- Black pepper: ¼- tsp or as per your taste

For Stuffing:

- Onion: 1- small diced
- Chicken: 1- cup
- Butter: 4- tbsp.
- Salt: ¼- tsp or as per your taste
- Black pepper: ¼- tsp or as per your taste

Instructions:

1. First preheat a mini waffle maker if needed & grease it. Then in a mixing bowl, add all the chaffle ingredients mix them all well

2. Then pour the mixture to the lower plate of the waffle maker & spread it evenly to cover the plate properly & close the lid

3. Now cook for at least 4 minutes to get the desired crunch and remove the chaffle from the heat & keep aside

4. Now make as many chaffles as your mixture & waffle maker allow. Take a small frying pan & melt butter in it on medium-low heat sauté chicken &onion & add salt & pepper

5. Then take another bowl & tear chaffles down into minute pieces. Then add chicken & onion to it

6. Then take a casserole dish, & add this new stuffing mixture to it Finally bake it at 350 degrees for around 30 minutes & serve hot.

38. Easy Chicken Vegetable Chaffles

Prep Time: 15-min | Total Time: 20-min |

Serve: 2

Ingredients:

For the Chaffle:

- 2- Egg
- Mozzarella Cheese: 1- cup (shredded)
- Salt: - a pinch

For the Chicken:

- Chicken pieces:- 2-4
- Ginger powder: ½- tbsp
- Salt: ¼- tsp or as per your taste
- Black pepper: ¼- tsp or as per your taste
- Cauliflower: 3 -tbsp
- Cabbage: 3- tbsp
- Green pepper: 1- tbsp
- Spring onion: 1- stalk

Instructions:

1. First boil the chicken, green pepper, cauliflower, & cabbage in a saucepan, when done strain the water

2. Then shred the chicken into small pieces & blend all the vegetables & mix them

3. Finely chop the spring onion & mix with the chicken & set aside preheat a mini waffle maker if needed & grease it

4. Then in a mixing bowl, add all the chaffle ingredients & mix well

5. Now pour a little amount of mixture to the lower plate of the waffle maker & spread it evenly to cover the plate properly

6. Now add the chicken mixture on top & again spread the thin layer of the mixture & close the lid

7. Then cook for at least 4 minutes to get the desired crunch to remove the chaffle from the heat

8. Finally, make as many chaffles as your mixture & waffle maker allow serve hot & enjoy

39. Cabbage Chicken Chaffle:

Prep Time: 15-min | Total Time: 25-min |

Serve: 2

Ingredients:

- Chicken:- 3-4 pieces or ½ -cup when done
- Soy Sauce: 1- tbsp
- Garlic: 2- clove
- Cabbage: 1- cup
- 2- Egg
- Mozzarella cheese: 1- cup
- Salt: As per your taste
- Black pepper: ¼- tsp or as per your taste
- White pepper: ¼- tsp or as per your taste

Instructions:

1. First, melt butter in oven or stove & set aside

2. Then in a pot, cook the chicken & cabbage by adding one cup of water to it with salt & bring to boil

3. Now close the lid of the pot & cook for 15-20 minutes

4. When done, remove from the stove & shred the chicken pieces leaving the bones behind; discard the bones

5. Now strain the water from cabbage and blend. grate garlic finely into pieces

6. Now in a small bowl, beat egg & mix chicken, cabbage, garlic, soy sauce, black pepper, & white pepper

7. Now mix all the ingredients well

8. Then preheat the waffle maker if needed & grease it

9. Now place around 1/8 cup of shredded mozzarella cheese to the waffle maker

10. Now pour the mixture over the cheese on the waffle maker & add 1/8 cup shredded cheese on top as well

11. Now cook for 4-5 minutes or until it is done

12. Finally, make as many chaffles as your mixture & waffle maker allow serve hot!

40. Chicken Zucchini Chaffle

Prep Time: 10-min | Total Time: 25-min |

Serve: 2

Ingredients:

- Chicken: 1- cup boneless pieces
- Zucchini: 1- (small)
- 2- Eggs
- Salt: as per your taste
- Shredded mozzarella: 1- cup
- Parmesan: 2- tbsp
- Pepper: as per your taste
- Basil: 1- tsp
- Water: ½ -cup

Instructions:

1. First, in a small saucepan, add chicken with a half cup of water & boil till chicken tenders

2. Now preheat your waffle iron grate zucchini finely

3. Now add all the ingredients to zucchini in a bowl &mix well. Then shred chicken finely & add it as well

4. Now grease your waffle iron lightly

5. Then pour the mixture into a full-size waffle maker & spread evenly. Now cook till it turns crispy

6. Finally, make as many chaffles as your mixture &waffle maker allow serve crispy and hot

41. Chicken Spinach Chaffle

Prep Time: 15-min | Total Time: 20-min |

Serve: 2

Ingredients:

Spinach: ½- cup

- Chicken: ½- cup boneless
- 1- Egg
- Shredded mozzarella: half cup
- Pepper: As per your taste
- Garlic powder: 1- tbsp
- Onion powder: 1- tbsp
- Salt: As per your taste
- Basil: 1- tsp

Instructions:

1. First, boil the chicken in water to make it tender then shred it into small pieces & set aside

2. Then boil spinach in a saucepan for 10 minutes & strain. Now preheat your waffle iron

3. Now add all the ingredients to boiled spinach in a bowl & mix well. now add the shredded chicken. Then grease your waffle iron lightly

4. Now pour the mixture into a full-size waffle maker & spread evenly. Now cook till it turns crispy

5. Finally, make as many chaffles as your mixture & waffle maker allow serve crispy & with your favorite keto sauce

42. Chicken BBQ Chaffle

Prep Time: 12-min | Total Time: 25-min | Serve: 2

Ingredients:

- Chicken: 1/2- cup
- Butter: 1- tbsp
- BBQ sauce: 1- tbsp (sugar-free)
- Almond flour: 2- tbsp
- 1- Egg
- Cheddar cheese: ½- cup

Instructions:

1. First cook the chicken in the butter on a low-medium heat for 10 minutes & preheat your waffle iron
2. Then in a mixing bowl, add all the chaffle ingredients including chicken & mix well
3. Then grease your waffle iron lightly

4. Now pour the mixture to the bottom plate evenly; also spread it out to get better results & close the upper plate & heat

5. Now cook for 6 minutes or until the chaffle is done

6. Finally, make as many chaffles as your mixture & waffle maker allow

43. Crispy Fried Chicken Chaffle

Prep Time: 15-min | Total Time: 5-min |

Serve: 2

Ingredients:

For Chaffle:

- 1 Egg
- Mozzarella Cheese: ½- cup (shredded)

For Fried Chicken:

- Chicken strips: 8- pieces
- Butter: 2- tbsp
- Salt: ¼- tsp or as per your taste
- Black pepper: ¼- tsp or as per your taste
- Red chili flakes: ½- tsp

Instructions:

1. First, in a frying pan, melt butter & fry chicken strips on medium-low heat add the spices at the & and set aside

2. Now mix all the chaffle ingredients well together and pour a thin layer on a preheated waffle iron

3. Then add chicken strips & pour again more mixture over the top cook the chaffle for around 5 minutes

4. Finally, make as many chaffles as your mixture & waffle maker allow serve hot!

Prep Time: 15-min | Total Time: 25-min |

Serve: 2

Ingredients:

- Canned chicken breast: ½- cup
- Onion powder: 1/8- tsp
- Garlic powder: 1/8- tsp
- 1- Eggs
- Cheddar cheese: ¼-cup
- Jalapeno: 1- diced
- Cream cheese: 1- tbsp
- Parmesan cheese: 1/8 -tbsp

Instructions:

1. First preheat a mini waffle maker if needed & grease it
2. Then in a mixing bowl, beat eggs & add all the ingredients mix them all well

3. Then pour the mixture to the lower plate of the waffle maker & spread it evenly to cover the plate properly

4. Now close the lid

5. Then cook for at least 4 minutes to get the desired crunch

6. Now remove the chaffle from the heat & keep aside for around one minute. Finally, make as many chaffles as your mixture & waffle maker allow

7. Then serve hot & enjoy!

45. Beef Teriyaki Avocado Chaffle Burger

Prep Time: 5-min | Total Time: 20-min |

Serve: 2

Ingredients:

For Chaffle:

- 2- Egg
- Mozzarella cheese: 1- cup (shredded)
- Avocado: half
- Green Leaf Lettuce: 2- leaves optional

For Patty:

- Ground Beef:½- lb Pork Panko:1-tbsp

Salt: ¼- tsp

- Egg:- 1
- Salt: ¼- tsp or as per your taste
- Black pepper: ¼- tsp or as per your taste

For Teriyaki Sauce:

- Japanese Sake: 2- tbsp
- Soy Sauce: 1- tbsp
- Xanthan Gum: 1/8- tsp
- Swerve/Monkfruit: 1- tbsp

Instructions:

1. First in a saucepan, add Japanese Sake, Soy Sauce, Xanthan Gum,& Swerve/Monkfruit & bring to boil on high heat

2. Then lower the heat and cook the mixture for a minute or two and mix continuously

3. When Xanthan Gum dissolves, remove from heat and let it cool. Take a mixing bowl and add ground beef, pork panko, egg, salt, and pepper, and mix with your hands

4. When the mixture becomes smooth, turn it into a ball and press it on a plate and make it a patty

5. A patty should be over ¼ inch thick and make sure to put your thumb in between the patty so that it doesn't expand upward and retains its shape

6. Preheat the grill to 350 degrees and cook the patties from both sides on medium to low heat for 4-5 minutes till patties turn brown

7. You can also use a frying pan to fry the patties. Preheat a mini waffle maker if needed

8. In a mixing bowl, beat eggs and add mozzarella cheese to them. Mix them all well and pour to the greasy mini waffle maker. Cook for at least 4 minutes to get the desired crunch

9. Remove the chaffle from the heat and keep aside

10. Make as many chaffles as your mixture and waffle maker allow. Cut avocado in slices

11. Wash green leaf lettuce and dry

12. Take two chaffles and arrange a beef patty with the slices of avocado, green lettuce, and teriyaki sauce in between to make a burger

13. Serve hot and enjoy

46. Sloppy Joe Chaffle

Prep Time: 15-min | Total Time: 25-min |

Serve: 2

Ingredients:

For Sloppy Joe:

- Ground beef: 1 lb

- Onion powder: 1 tsp

- Tomato paste: 3 tbsp

- Garlic: 1 tsp (minced)

- Chili powder: 1 tbsp

- Cocoa powder: 1 tbsp

- Bone broth: ½ cup

- Coconut Aminos: 1 tsp (soy sauce could be used instead)

- Mustard powder: 1 tbsp

- Paprika: ½ tsp

- Swerve brown: 1 tsp

- Salt: ¼ tsp or as per your taste

- Black pepper: ¼ tsp or as per your taste

For Cornbread Chaffle:

- Egg: 1
- Cheddar cheese: ½ cup
- Jalapeno: 5 slices (diced)
- Corn extract: ¼ tsp
- Salt: ¼ tsp or as per your taste
- Franks red hot sauce: 1 tsp

Instructions:

1. In a saucepan, add ground beef and sprinkle salt and pepper first. Now add all the other ingredients and let it simmer
2. Preheat a mini waffle maker if needed and grease it
3. In a mixing bowl, beat eggs and add cheddar cheese to them with the remaining ingredients

4. Pour the mixture to the lower plate of the waffle maker and spread it evenly to cover the plate properly and close the lid

5. Cook for at least 4 minutes to get the desired crunch. Remove the chaffle from the heat

6. Make as many chaffles as your mixture and waffle maker allow. Add the warm Sloppy Joe on top

7. Serve hot and enjoy!

47. Beef Strips Chaffle

Prep Time: 10-min | Total Time: 25-min |

Serve: 2

Ingredients:

For Chaffle:

- Egg: 1
- Mozzarella Cheese: ½ cup (shredded)
- Salt: ¼ tsp or as per your taste
- Black pepper: ¼ tsp or as per your taste
- Ginger powder: 1 tbsp

For Beef Strips:

- Beef strips: 8 pieces
- Butter: 2 tbsp
- Salt: ¼ tsp or as per your taste
- Black pepper: ¼ tsp or as per your taste
- Red chili flakes: ½ tsp

Instructions:

1. In a frying pan, melt butter and fry beef strips on medium-low heat. Add water to make them tender and boil for 30 minutes

2. Add the spices at the end and set aside. Mix all the chaffle ingredients well. Pour a thin layer on a preheated waffle iron

3. Add beef strips and pour again more mixture over the top. Cook the chaffle for around 5 minutes

4. Make as many chaffles as your mixture and waffle maker allow. Serve hot with your favorite sauce.

48. Beef BBQ Chaffle

Prep Time: 15-min | Total Time: 25-min | Serve: 2

Ingredients:

- Beef mince: 1/2 cup
- Butter: 1 tbsp
- BBQ sauce: 1 tbsp (sugar-free)
- Almond flour: 2 tbsp
- Egg: 1
- Cheddar cheese: ½ cup

Instructions:

1. Cook the beef mince in the butter and half cup water on a low-medium heat for 20 minutes
2. Then increase the flame to reduce water. Preheat your waffle iron

3. In mixing bowl, add all the chaffle ingredients including beef mince, and mix well

4. Grease your waffle iron lightly

5. Pour the mixture to the bottom plate evenly; also spread it out to get better results and close the upper plate and heat

6. Cook for 6 minutes or until the chaffle is done.

7. Make as many chaffles as your mixture and waffle maker allow.

49. Beef Eggplant Chaffle

Prep Time: 15-min | Total Time: 20-min |

Serve: 2

Ingredients:

For Chaffles:

- Eggs: 2
- Cheddar cheese: ½ cup
- Parmesan cheese: 2 tbsp
- Italian season: ¼ tsp
- Beef mince: 1 cup

For Eggplant:

- Eggplant: 1 big
- Salt: 1 pinch
- Black pepper: 1 pinch
- Red chili flakes: 1/2 tsp

Instructions:

1. Cook the beef mince with half cup water on medium-low flame for 20 minutes

2. Increase the flame afterward to remove excess water. Cut the eggplant in slices and boil in water and strain Add a pinch of salt and pepper with red chili flakes

3. Add all the chaffle ingredients in a bowl and mix well to make a mixture

4. Add the boiled beef

5. Preheat a mini waffle maker if needed and grease it

6. Pour the mixture to the lower plate of the waffle maker and spread it evenly to cover the plate properly

7. Add the eggplant about two slices on the mixture and cover the lid. Cook for at least 4 minutes to get the desired crunch

8. Remove the chaffle from the heat

9. Make as many chaffles as your mixture and waffle maker allow

Prep Time: 10-min | Total Time: 25-min |

Serve: 2

Ingredients:

For Chaffle:

- Egg: 2
- Mozzarella Cheese: ½ cup (shredded)
- Garlic powder: ¼ tsp
- Salt: ¼ tsp or as per your taste
- Black pepper: ¼ tsp or as per your taste

For Stuffing:

- Onion: 1 small diced
- Beef mince: 1 cup
- Butter: 4 tbsp
- Salt: ¼ tsp or as per your taste
- Black pepper: ¼ tsp or as per your taste

Instructions:

1. Preheat a mini waffle maker if needed and grease it in a mixing bowl, add all the chaffle ingredients Mix them well

2. Pour the mixture to the lower plate of the waffle maker and spread it evenly to cover the plate properly and close the lid

3. Cook for at least 4 minutes to get the desired crunch. Remove the chaffle from the heat and keep aside

4. Make as many chaffles as your mixture and waffle maker allow. Take a small frying pan and melt butter in it on medium-low heat Sauté beef mince and onion and add salt and pepper

5. Cook for over 20 minutes

6. Take another bowl and tear chaffles down into small pieces. Add beef and onion to it

7. Take a casserole dish, and add this new stuffing mixture to it Bake it at 350 degrees for around 30 minutes and serve hot.

FAQs

Is it compatible with special diets?

VEGETARIAN DIET

The ketogenic chaffle diet is compatible with a wide vegetarian diet, excluding only meats and allowing the consumption of eggs, fish, and seafood.

VEGAN DIET

The ketogenic chaffle diet, which will exclude grains and pulses, is not compatible with a balanced vegan diet. Combining the two diets would amount to eating only oleaginous fruits, seeds, oils, and vegetables and can lead to multiple deficiencies like protein, calcium, vitamins D, and B12.

GLUTEN-FREE DIET

The ketogenic chaffle diet will exclude the main foods that may contain gluten: cereals and cooked industrial foods (dishes, soups, sauces, etc.). It is compatible with a gluten-free diet, provided that you check the composition of certain products, such as cold cuts or minced steaks, in which gluten can be used as a texture agent.

LOW SALT DIET

The ketogenic chaffle diet will exclude major sources of salt: bread and commercial ready meals. It is compatible with a low-salt diet provided you limit deli meats, all types of cheese, smoked or canned fish, canned vegetables, salted nuts, and cooking salt.

KOSHER DIET

The ketogenic chaffle diet is compatible with a kosher diet, provided that you consume kosher meat and stick to authorized meats and fish.

HALAL DIET

The ketogenic chaffle diet is compatible with a halal diet, provided that you consume halal meat, stick to authorized meats, and avoid commercial products containing the additives E 120, E 471, and E 472.

Are the benefits of this diet sufficient?

The macronutrient intakes of the ketogenic chaffle diet are very far from the recommended intakes.

Contribution to total energy intake in a ketogenic chaffle diet:

Lipid intake: 70 to 80%

Carbohydrate intake: 5 to 10%

Protein intake: 10 to 20%

Contribution to total energy intake according to the recommendations for the French or European population:

Lipid intake: 35 to 40%

Carbohydrate intake: 40 to 55%

Protein intake: 10 to 20%

The medium to long term consequences of such diets on health is not known. The weight loss with increased fat intake and reduced carbohydrate consumption raises cardiovascular risks according to some reports.

The ketogenic chaffle diet, excluding cereals and strongly restricting fruits and vegetables, lacks fiber, which also contributes to constipation. Additionally, fiber is one of the preventive nutrients for cardiovascular disease and some cancers and maintains a great balance in the intestinal flora (many studies explain a relationship between unbalanced microbiota and increased risk of different diseases).

Owing to the restriction in fruits and vegetables, there is also a scarcity of vitamin C, beta-carotene, and polyphenols in the ketogenic chaffle diet (compounds with antioxidant or anti-inflammatory properties that might not be present in food supplements except for a few, because they are more than 2000).

Overall, the ketogenic chaffle diet does not provide sufficient protective nutrients (useful in the prevention of the most common diseases, such as cardiovascular disease or cancer) for long-term follow-up. Food supplements recommended by a doctor or advised by nutritionists may be consumed after following this diet.

What type of meal does this diet offer?

Example Of A Typical Day Providing 1500 Kcal

BREAKFAST:

Unsweetened coffee or tea;

30 g (1 handful) almonds, walnuts or hazelnuts;

50 g of red fruits: strawberries, raspberries, blackcurrants.

LUNCH AND DINNER:

50 g of raw vegetables (the equivalent of a small grated carrot), vinaigrette with 1 tablespoon of walnut or rapeseed oil;

120 g of meat or fish or 2 eggs: cooking with 1 tablespoon of rapeseed or olive oil;

100 g cooked vegetables (1 small plate), with 20 g (2 teaspoons) of butter or 60 g (2 tablespoons) of the whole cream.

TO TASTE:

60 g (the equivalent of 1/4 of camembert) of cheese OR 30 g of cheese and 100 g (1 ramekin) of whole milk cottage cheese.

Ketogenic chaffle diet: how to avoid deviations and manage runway excursions?

It doesn't matter in which phase of a ketogenic chaffle diet you are either with fewer than 20 g of carbohydrates per day or in a long-term keto chaffle diet with up to 50 g of carbohydrates allowed your journey can easily end. A croissant, a sandwich, or a beer and this could be the end of the road.

Disadvantage: You must allow re-entering ketosis for a period of 3 to 7 days. You need to be consistent to achieve your goal.

The long-term, keto-adaptation must be the only target the keto chaffle diet follower should be seeking. But even by targeting this way of eating for the long term, from a social point of view, it seems useful to be able to eat a meal without restriction, or even to resume a more traditional diet for a time. The ideal is to be able to plan it according to its targets in advance.

I'm out: how do I stick to my ketogenic chaffle diet?

Often a real challenge can be eating a ketogenic chaffle diet.

As much as this diet is considered to be the least restrictive that you have been given to follow, as sometimes there are more difficult moments than others, especially festive meals, restaurant outings, invitations to friends or family.

When you're invited to an aperitif, you can still bring a platter of cold meats and cheese. You're not going empty-handed and you won't finish on an empty stomach, above all. The challenge often arises at dessert during a meal. If the cheese platter is fortunately very well supplied, take advantage of it at that time by choosing those which support very low levels of carbohydrate (most). Please note, however, during the induction phase milk products are to be eaten in fairly small amounts.

When dessert is being served just keep a low profile and say you are no longer hungry, or simply clarify why you are missing it.

I'm stagnating: Keto Plateau…how to avoid?

Those individuals who opt for ketogenic chaffle diet for weight loss, there may be some frustrating periods; fat loss doesn't always lead to weight loss.

There are a few ways to get out of those stages of stagnation or plateau.

One of the methods to help keep the weight loss going is to take a snapshot of what you're going to eat so you don't consume much, and you're going to get a good estimate of the calories.

Too much calorie intake probably induces stagnation, even though the macro distribution is respected and ketosis mounted. Meal calories can be decreased by using low-calorie ingredients (pickles, konjac, etc.) or by testing the diet for mindfulness.

Additionally, there are also other tips:
Drink a full glass of water before each meal,
Eating without distraction, without disturbance, without television, just eat slowly,

Try to grasp all the elements: colors, texture, flavors, smells, constantly look for signs of satiety.

Keto in stingy mode: how to follow a ketogenic chaffle diet without breaking the bank?

Another challenge of this diet emerges very rapidly: the basic items like salmon, duck, shrimp that are used in the menus are costly and the bill increases exponentially.

In the long term, this increase in food prices is to be complicated by the reduction in quantities, proteins, and especially lipids that allow satiety to be reached more quickly. You can modify your diet according to the availability of the food items.

CONCLUSION

The ketogenic diet does not represent a miracle diet. It could have as its aim to help people lose weight. But, above all, it aims to create over time a new way of nourishing. Because the change is quite radical compared to what we usually consume. And in the long run, that's not easy. Olivia Charlet also recommends being followed by an expert trained in ketogenic food to support this change and, of course, even more, if one adopts this mode of food to improve one's health.

If you're not careful, the Keto chaffle diet will yield dangerous results.

Initially, one may feel uncomfortable (headache, tiredness, nausea), the time the body adjusts to the lack of glucose and succeeds in generating fat energy. Cutting out certain categories of food can lead to certain deficiencies like fiber, vitamins, and minerals.

The ingestion of too many animal products is detrimental to health (chronic inflammation, increased cancer risk including colon risk). The reason Olivia Charlet suggests adopting a hypoxic ketogenic diet that is without excess meat and dairy products is that this diet is safer and can be helpful to certain people.

Printed in Great Britain
by Amazon

22445997R00090